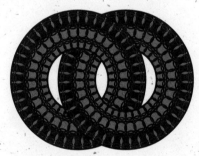

GlOrious

POEMS

JOAN CUSACK HANDLER

CavanKerry ◊ Press LTD.

Library of Congress Cataloging-in-Publication Data

Handler, Joan Cusack, 1941–
      Glorious: poems / Joan Cusack Handler.
                    p. cm.
        ISBN 0-9707186-4-0
          I. Title

    PS3608.A7 G58 2002
    811'.6–dc21   2001058323

Cover art: "Fondo" ©1998 by Carlos Andrade
Cover art property of Leo Malca, Malca Fine Arts, New York
Cover and interior design by Rafael Attias

First Edition

Printed in the United States of America

CavanKerry Press Ltd.
Fort Lee, New Jersey
www.cavankerrypress.com

For the nest of us:
          Alan, my husband
     & David, our son

                                        & for Molly Peacock,
                         Earth & GodmOther of my poems

CONTENTS

The Spirit Speaking Its Exegesis

by Afaa Michael Weaver

> The only way I can take you back, Lord
> is if we agree   that you're just
> another parent...
> —"Between Parents"

Glorious takes the broad and dangerous campaign into the heart of betrayal and loss, dangerous inasmuch as humanity would rather not believe the deepest depths of its own cruelty, the way it seeks its own ending by murdering its promise. It takes a lifetime to live, if that living is to be a full realization of the truth of our lives, and all too often we have not a lifetime. We have no chance to get at the true light but are only here to make deposits—to sing brief songs. The aria in this collection is a pain so named for the poet's time spent wandering and then, in a blessing, reclaiming the dead parts of a self, the dead who breathe love's failure. In this shimmering collection, Joan Handler shows us the gems that come from pain in the fragile fibers of her spirit, as the poems fall like pearls fleeing their binding strings to be reborn. In this making, the poet gathers a harmony with the internal and external spirits of her life, naming suffering and concepts of a God for what they are, the necessary but flawed entities in a universe we name as our own.

The page becomes the broad space of breathing in compositions that draw images forming the trace of a spirit's navigation of the air rather than the visual suggestiveness of ordinary concrete poetry. These are images guided by the fountainhead of a burgeoning self-awareness that came of its own accord to the poet. The collection is therefore a vatic lyricism. It reveals its inner sight, the sight of a woman writing out of an assumption of basic victories. So this is not a feminist reconstructing and revaluing of the self per se, but it is rather a song that assumes a female sanctity and goes on to roll back other stones from other caverns of another City of the Oppressed, namely the inner world of women growing out of their own self-defined context, one that has assumed its own sanctity and legit-imacy on many levels so that they can visit the hall of mirrors in which we all live.

In "Stuff It," Handler writes, "Anger is All I ever wanted." It is an anger that flies out and becomes the maker of the art of flying. To her body she says, "...I promise you more / attention." In the spaces between poems the power gathers itself and demands that the world be a place full and wise enough to know the depth of a woman's pain arising from the first evil in life, the murdering of a child's spir-it and the deepening of that wound, the oppressive conspiracy against a woman's blossoming that is rooted in fears shared by men and women. Writing of her mother's failure and of her own engaging of reality, Handler summons courage in the reader, much in the tradition of poets who write out of life's deepest terrors. The reader's courage is to be admired. The poet's courage is to be honored in song because it requires the undoing of a life in order to love. Handler writes the full orchestral score of what is *female*. It is a song as vibrant as the visible sky and the starry night on which it hangs.

The primal gesture of liberation for a woman, naming and reclaiming her body, is the second part of the dynamic of this collection, one that propels itself toward light's speed and thus its essence in nam-ing a little girl, naming her through sight and vision. The poet's recollection is that of a human being watching its own assemblage from the difficult parts of a life that lie about liked a mixed media sculp-ture. There is the dried blood of tears that turn crimson with time. There is a fierceness here that tran-scends Sexton and Plath's despair, and there is a revelry in the musicality of the page as canvas that avoids both the opaque difficulty of Olson and the formless and inverted play of the failures of jazz-inspired lines. In "Bad," Handler writes of the vaginal image, singing self-love, "The V at the body's center: / those who shrunk from it...those who couldn't wait to touch it." *Glorious* discovers and names the centers in a way that shows us how this love, initiated by a remembrance of all the complexities of pain, yields to further decentering, as the poet's song begins to sing serenity. Serenity, of course, can only begin in navigating sincerity. Handler shows a precious knowledge, namely that a journey to serenity often has no map except courage.

Moving between excavation of memory and pirouettes in the center of pain and revelry, the poems crest and dip in a teleological way to their summation that is an energetic correspondent to the general topography of each piece in the collection. The spirit of the book lives as the poet lives, seeking and then knowing and seeking again. There is the pain of the spirit recollected in a moment of recognition and acceptance, and from there the poems move into the physical pain. Handler writes of the misfortunes of falling, as if the falling is an unavoidable tumbling into the consummate wisdom of the spirit and of the body. "Pain is the cage I can't climb out of /... It's the only life I feel / these four months / ...since I missed my step, fell &..."

In "Psychotherapist with Black Leather Binder Sits in White Oak Chair that Came through a Fire," Handler writes "I do God's work here. / People bring their marriages, ...saints & demons, mothers & fathers, / the cloaks of their shame." It is as if the humility deepened by remembrance is further deepened and battered into shimmering light with physical pain, as along the way she tosses away the cloak of shame.

In introducing Joan Handler's *Glorious*, I welcome a poetry collection embracing the rarest truth, the truth that takes us into the essence of light, beyond the appreciable perimeters of that miracle that makes it possible for us to see.

July 2002
Somerville, Massachusetts

GlOrious

Pageant of Rages

It is pure genius & a running away of the heart

that frees us   out here

in front of the Cathedral of St. John the Divine,

two elegant women hissing obscenities

at each other: delicious as the chocolates

with cherry

centers

o o zing

lush & bloody rages.

Mother & daughter-in-law   spitting hate

feeling grateful

& loving each other for it.

And maybe it is God

& His Friends

or our own generosity

that sends us parading through the vestibule

through the stench of too much old skin,

incense & hair

gathering the drunk, the sorry & the heartless

& the lost souls at the end of the hall.

After trading our street clothes for green

gowns & turbans,

we empty the chapels,

calling to us   the woman on her knees muttering to the Virgin,

the girl in white gloves

lighting candles   & the old guy

with the leaking eyes.   Then

down Morningside Drive

across   Amsterdam   to   Broadway,   we   P a r a d e   our
P A G E A N T   o f   R A G E S ,   H u n
- d r e d s   o f   HAppy,   raVing   c o r p s e s :

our hair from our turbans

a wilderness of wirefloodingthestreets,

noses & toenails

stretching to

points,

the fleshy softness

of forearms   melting   to the

cold   white

outline

of   bone.

In the mirrors of cars & storefront windows,

I watch with admiration   as

my eyes flare   hOt & glassy

at the sight of you;

Del*i*rious with f**u**ry, I

p*E*acock   & raising my dress up over my thighs,

I kick the top off a manhole, get my feet

stuck

in the stinking tar

& fall onmyface spittingSUCK!   PuTZ!   *WHORE!*

CocKsucker!Asshole!

Then red, raw, more ravishing than ever you rise   up   hOwling *SLUT!*

You're not fit to be any*one's daughter!*

You're no Mother! I spit

*You h**a**te your children!*   Bitch!

bellows the old guy with the leaking eyes.

WhOre !   One for my side from the woman gAping from the fourth floor window.

                                                    Your house is a PIG STY!

                                    Your husband is Pussywhipped!

                Your children Hate you!   from the Lady muttering to the Virgin.

        Today we celebrate: two

                        short months & I'll be

                                    sitting beside you

                                        begging you not to

                                                    die

                                                        (& half meaning it!)

                                bitching as I do about your selfishness—

                                                                                    leaving

                                            without a word.

        But today we'll be generous:

                        we'll not let go

                            without   saying what we have to.

                                                            Today

        our husbands

        & sons

    have no wives or mothers:

                            only   two hairy **P**etticoats

spinning

            a

                l**o**vers   TiRade.

———

5

I acted like someone who couldn't be trusted, she said.
Each year when hurricane season hit,
I stood at the window
waiting for the river to swell into the street.
& it never scared me. I wanted it
wilder. Soon as she turned around &   the whistling
stopped   & the rain no longer smashed itself against the windows,
I sneaked out to swim in the streets,
then checked out the neighborhood
in our canoe.   I loved
s *peed* too !
she caught me once on the back of a HARLEY at   **9   0**
scrE*aming***FAS***T***ER***!
I am the body she lives in.

She bitches about You, Lord,
but with all her preaching
about accepting one's
children, she never
loved me.
She never took her eyes off me.
She locked me in my room.
She refused to let me   wander
even in the yard. She was so
convinced I'd rush Out
w i ld as a wEed & promiScuous.
She was afraid I had   B I g   Plans,
suspected me   of   wanting   to   be   a   G   I   A   N   T
—recognized early on
how   g   r   e   e   d   y   I   was   howmuchofa
rushIwasin

6

thr0wing

fingers

&

     toes

like

branches.

So she dwarfed me.

Just listen to her
comments about
bonsai—how she
cuts, prunes &
shapes me
rather than

let *me*

have the room

to decide for myself

how   GRAND   I   want   to   be,   how   f a r   I   want   to

thr0w   a   limb.

Like all rejecting parents,
    she kept our war
        to herself: faking
           l o v e
           outside,
           forcingmeinto
           thecloset
           athome.

She kept me in dark clothes & no mirrors
& made believe I wasn't there.

Still she fooled everyone

Walking   Head   High   —   Gaze   Right   Out   There   With   The   Leaves.

I'll bet you thought she was proud.
But she wasn't.
She hated me.

Everyone else admired our size.
Our piano teachers flipped
over our l0ng fingers.   We had
plenty of room in our biceps &
thighs to   thr0w out
p o u nds   of muscle
& I always was attracted to a muscular bacK.
I saw nothing wrong with big shoulders either.

I'm still pissed about the swimming—
she breezed through
Water Safety (the only girl in a class with **11** guys!)
Was I Proud!
Swam easily
5 0   - 6 0   l   a   p   s   a day
'til the coach said,   *Time to lift weights.*
No way !   I'll look like a fuLLBack, she said.

Well, everyone knows about neglected children—
how some turn out bad,
still others get even.
So   the more she disowned me,

8

the harder I made it for her—

thr0wing e v e r y thing in her path;
she couldn't walk
without breaking a limb.
I even refused
to
grow
a
straight
spine

did lots
of
fancy
twists
&
turns
'til her
back
was
inconsolable.
It got so
she couldn't stop
thinking of me—
trying to buy me off
with massages &
vitamins &
trips to specialists.   But
I just kept going—

She liked small?

Well,Iconcoctedthis
tinybladderthat
wouldn'tservicea
threeyearold,so
everytimeshegets
comfortable,
shehastopiss.

Embarrasses the hell out of her.
Sure takes the edge off sex.

She thought we had different values?
She was right.
I didn't care about fitting in
& hiding
or stupid boyfriends
or being small, blond
& busty.
I didn't care
about the teasing—
Mom was right.
The other kids were just jealous.

It wouldn't have bothered *me*
to fly out a b o v e the others.   An inch or   2,
f i v e   o r   s i x   for that matter.

I was prepared to **re**ally make a StaTemenT.

But she treated me
like   the kid
who hangs out
the window
sure   she   can   *f* l y,
so   she chained me to the bed.

Truth is,
she knew

if she left me
alone   even for a minute,
I *would have*

s   p   r   e   a   d

my

W   I   N   G   S   &   T   A

k   e   n   o   f   **F**

Hot & w *i* l d as Rosalba's chili,   ANGER paRades   in purple patent
pumps & an *o*rgy of R   i   b   **b**   o   *n*   S   blanket the floor.
She has long black lashes & emerald
lids, strawberry lips & cheeks, &
around her neck, she wears
tiger eye,
marcasite,
amethyst,
turquoise&
diamonds.

Nothing is to**o** much for *A*nger.

Anger is Absug
Conducting
a Choir of F Sharp*S*.
Sunday mornings, she's a g*i*ddy feast o f   g   u   l   l   s
at the East Hampton Dump. Anger is
a huge red parachute,
a hot air Balloon,
& a beanstalk that shOOts up like Jack's did.
Like money for candy, I can never have
enough.   I've lived so long without,
w**a**nting it
but a*fraid* of it,
I will **N**ever get used to Anger.   I L**O**ve my *A*NGER.

Open the Door!
I'll fill the house with It
with enough left over for the
nuns & priests.

                                                            Anger is a HU*RR*ICANE,
                    roofstornoff&   flung
        down the river.
                It's a superstore of chocolates & pizza,   silk coats
                                    for every party, pedicures each night. Anger is
                    failing e v e r y thing one month
                                        then Acing the next.
                It's a crowd of cantors at 6 A.M. Mass.
                                            It's perfumed nuns in low cut dresses
                                    winking at priests.
                It's Kafka & Bankers & idiot saVants,
                                        Mussolini & Mozart, Warhol & Tevye,
                & a h u g e Ice Cream Sundae painted by Van Gogh
                    Anger is
    s t r o l l i n g t h r o u g h a s t o r e, taking what you want withoutstoppingtopay.
            It's sleeping in the desert,
                            coyotes to soothe you,   then wailing in the forest
                                    with a chorus of black crows.
    Anger is *resentment,*
            irritation, aggravation, exasperation,
                                vexation, indignation, animosity, wrath &
                                        bitterness. Infuriated,
                                                it's *ire, mad, temper,*

            dander,
            pique,
            stew,   *huff, tiff, miff,*
                        conniption,
                        paroxysm,

rage, passion, fit....   Anger is *Shit, Piss, Fuck,*
                                        Asskisser, Cocksucker,
                                            Cunt, Dick, Putz,
                                  Asshole,Dildo, Pussy,Suck,WhOre!

The eleventh commandment
                preached by my father, my mother,
                the doctor & nuns, my best friends'
                            grandpa
                & the Yo-Yo King:
                                        Thou Shalt NOT *Be Angry!*

    Like the fat woman in her girdle, I
                learned well to stuff it. Find a pocket or cave;
                        there's room
                behind the rib cage or inside
                            the breasts.
                                        But now   it's out there!

        Batten Down the HatcheS!

    Anger is All I ever wanted.

14

Perfect

PERFECT

I   CONFESSION

She is smart.
She knows:
to be loved, she must be
                    smart, so she
                        studies & gets good grades, a nervous stomach&COLITIS at nine.
She is holy
& sinless, but she
            doesn't know it; she
                        tries so
                        hard   not to be bad.
                                                    She follows her father to Mass
                                                            each morning
                            Saturdays at dusk, she
                                            k
                                            n
                                            e e l s for
                                            Confession.

            She c o n c e n t r ates
            on a l l the sins   she
            must have committed—
                            Disobeyed her mother?
                                She can't
                                think
                                        of an instance, but
                                        she musthave—
                                        Perhaps in her
                                        thoughts.
                                        She's sure
                                        she's had

Unkind thoughts — everyone
has
unkind
thoughts — she'll
include them.

What about
*Imp**u**re* thoughts?
She's never even tempted.

Lies?   She doesn't think so,
but how can anyone
be sure?   No
problem with Killing,
of course, no Stealing or
Coveting: she gives away
whatever she gets.
She moves closer
to the dark
green drape
&
p
r
i
e
- *d i e u* & the priest
with no face but
his kind cello voice
calling her,   *Child*.

Reviewing her list, she
eliminates:
        confessing sins   you *haven't* committed   could be Lying.

   She is so careful
      about lying.   No.
                                  No sin of
               disobedience.

               She does all she is told
               to: follows her brother
               & sister from school
               & tells their mother
               what she's been told to.
               She learns to cook &
               takes over the kitchen
               when her Mom goes to
               work. She warms milk
               & sifts flour as a priest
               might, preparing The
               Eucharist at First Mass.
               Summertime, she makes
               macaroni with cheese,
               & lettuce & tomato
               with mayonnaise &
               ketchup & Toll House
               cookies for dessert
                                      then she walks to the beach
               & calls her brothers for lunch.   *Bless me, Father*
for I have sinned....   For your Penance, say...

19

Her bed is on the right side
next to the wall.
It is always
messywithbooks&uniforms,
wrinkledwhiteblouses&longblacksocks.

She h a t es her
bed. It is always c o l   d,
wet & smelly.
She is twelve
& s t i l l she wets her bed.
Her mother tries to break her of this
Filthy habit
(The Doctor calls it that.
It is not her kidneys:
She is just a DIRTY PIG!
Her Mom defends her
later — says he is mean & they won't
go to him again.
She buys her new shoes).
But
after that, Mom makes her
wash her sheets   before school
each day.   So she d r a g s her   S   h   a   m   e
like Great Beaten Gulls the   l   e   n   g   t   h   of the house   through the kitchen
where the other three eat breakfast.
Her sister & younger brother
bow their heads.
They tend to be kind.   But
Sonny laughs loud & wild

as he watches her k

                n

                e

                e

ling before the claw footed tub.   She

                        isn't permitted to

                        close the door. Or

                                  use hot water.

        Icy water might teach her.

                      It is part of the training;

                          the Doctor has

                          taught her

                          Mother well:

You're the Mother!

                *Make her st**o**p this!*

    The father tries too.

    He carries her piggy

           - back

      to the bathroom at bedtime each night.

                            It is her favorite time of day.

                She is the first one   to get

                    so close to Dad. Dad doesn't

                      use his body

                      for holdingor touch.   He keeps it

for work

& prayer.   These evening rides

                are rauCous: with laughing &

                    SQU*EAL*ing & the other t h r e e

                             w a i t i n g

                                     in

                                 line.

She is
n o t small.
She is bare-
lythirteen &
she's t
a
l
l   as a *Woman.*
But
she has no Breasts

Two peas on an ironing board!

Sonny always laughs.   So she
never really
Looks like
a woMan.
Not girl either.
She is
something   in between.
She wonders   what it
would be
tobesmall.

She dreams of hiding,

imagines
walking
with   a sheet
covering
her face

&

G

I

G

a

n

t

i

c

body.

Then she could have   secrets:
things you do   that no-
body   sees.

The commandments are easy.

They're Sins,
Pure & Simple.   & if you break them
intentionally,   then die
that very minute
without confessing them, you go Straight to

HELL!   So definitions are important.
What's MORTAL?   Venial?

Even venial means burning
but Purgatory,
not Hell &
years
instead of
forever.

The good people go to Purgatory.

But The FIRE
still
scares her, so she's
careful
to commit as few sins
as possible
(& venial of course!)

But she worries about
her family, so she watches them carefully.
She worries over Sonny:
the Smoking & the Stealing
& those *Girlie* Magazines!

Even though he torments her,
she wouldn't want him to
go to Hell. He might grow out of it.
Besides,
sometimes he's nice.

So in Religion, one morning,
she asks Sr. Mary Thomas
what Drunk is
(Sonny's always bragging he gets **drunk** Friday nights.)
Sister proceeds with God's Assurance, *You are* Mortally Sinfully
DRUNK *when you can't get the key in the door*
on the <u>first</u> try!   She's afraid
for Sonny   & people like her
Uncle who seems *naturally*
clumsy.
She hopes ·
God will
take that into account &
give them an extra try.   But
she lies awake   nights now,
worrying about her
father last Christmas:
her mother had been angry
& he was vomiting in the
bathroom & later crying &
saying he was sorry to the
mother & all the kids.
So he *must have* confessed it.
He would **nev**er
let a thing like that
go by.

Greedy for any small sacrifice,
she counts
peach slices into dishes,
then serves
herself a few pieces
less. She offersherself up
to Sonny's
taunting &
gives away her
blue taffeta dress.
Jesus will love her best.

Studying the pose
of cloisteredsisters
who watch with Him
in the dark, she
tries to be quiet as a
painting: her hands &
face, unbearably white
&   drained of Earth.
Soon
He is   there
hovering
just slightly
over her shoulder   Yes, Lord,
I will be Yours.
I love
the thought of
the two of us
together always....

I sit back
in our empty chapel
& let You
come
down
upon me
from the altar,
the air inhere
upclose
tomyskin, its
safe
prayer
rising
from inside
that gold
tabernacle
door...Lord ! Youhaveme!
After all, You made me.

But
somedays she
envies girls who smoke
behind the Shrine, or curse
or stay out late &
never go to Daily Mass.
They're not worried about
God
calling *them* to be a nun.
At first she wonders why
anyone would *will* to be bad.
She can't imagine
anyone wanting to sin.
She isn't even tempted.
It's not that she is Perfect—
No one is Perfect   but God;
the next is her
father,
the Nuns,
then maybe her mother.   But
she wishes *she* was.
She works for it,
following
every
instruction.   But
these girls, & her
brother & sister, don't even
want to be.   That
confuses her.   Sonny
st0le

Mom's change &
he & their sister Catherine
smoke cigarettes
(he started at nine, he brags,
hiding them
under
the cellar
stairs).
& Mom found *Girlie* pictures
under his bed!   She overheard
Mom crying &   using words the
Doctor used
like di**sg**usting &
Filthy & DIRTY **P**IG &
something about sh*a*me & **S**ick
&...*Sisters living in the House!*

Then she threatened him:
Dad must never find out.

Sonny started living in the cellar after that.
He d r a g g e d
his
mattress
down
the
stairs
one
day
while their Mom was
still at work.

That's Sonny.

She's never understood

the things he does

like when he t h r o ws his

oatmeal

down

behind

the fridge

when their Mom turns

her back.

He does this when the milk goes bad

& Mom insists

it's fine &

says they'll eat it for dinner

if they don't for breakfast.

But she envies him

when he shows Mom his

empty plate &   leaves *her*

alone (& retching) at the table.

She's afraid of him

&wants to be his friend

but he says

she's a j0ke.

He makes her Swear she'll

never tell Anyone

she is his sister.

But she's changing:
   not rebellious, of course, just
      a bit less eager.   She
            feels guilty not wanting to
                   k
                   n
                   eel for the Rosary,   but
     she's happiest
    when she is sick &
can sit in a chair.

       She's never gotten used to kneeling.

       Everything centers on kneeling.

SATAN COMES IN

I

SATAN   is   EVERYWHERE.
He watches me
in the bathroom
then follows me to the cellar &
hangs   on the ceiling   those
nights   Mom
sends me down there to
iron or fold laundry, & he
spies on me from behind
the sheets that
hang   like

gh0st
cloaks
on the line.
I hear him SHRIEKing
in the voices of Devils
SONNY invents
when he knows
I am down there.

& SATAN
waits   in my bed room:
inbackofmy closet   behind
the shoes,
under the
uniforms
piled on my
bed, in the folds

                    of the blanket inside my
            mattress! undermy
                    pillow!
                            Summers he hides in
                                the wake of the barges&
                                        calls me
                        from under the
                lighthouse.   & last year SONNY said
                                            SATAN put
                                                Devils
                                                under all
                                            the buoys!

        But scariest of all — he's getting **in**to
                            my mind &isfillingin
                    thespaces*betweenmyprayers*!

                                            Now I go to the cellar
                                            only whenMom<u>makes</u>me,
                                        then only with my
                                    sister or little brother.
                At bedtime I   t   o   s   s
                                        pillows&
                blankets
        to surprise him.
        I don't swim out anymore   to the L i g h T house   or   bargeS & no longer   c   a
    - n o e to   C i t y   I s land.

                            But my mind is different.
                            It wOn't stop Thinking!

I pray so hard for heaven,
I know you have to *Intent*ionally
commit **Mortals** to become
SATAN's.   Of course
intentional means you don't have to
do it, you can only plan to —
dAydream,   even for a minute,
of sin.

It's the mind you have to   be afraid of.

Because once you decide to do It,
even if you don't, you've
<u>SINNED</u>.
Make sure the thought
never entersyour mind
because once it enters,
you could all of a suddenstart
thinking
about doing it, like **K**illing
some
-one,   even
your brother — *Oh,GOD!*
AmIdoingIT?!

But that one is easy —

we don't have
M U R D E R
in our house.   It's the PRIDE
& the Coveting
that're toughest.

There are six of us &
neverenough
potroastatsupperor
spacesintheconver-
sationsotheonlyway
to avoid the coveting
is to give away
my share &
offer it up for the Poor Souls
in Purgatory
who are always waiting &
can do nothing
for themselves.
It's a good thing I think
to make friends with the Souls.
They might remember
when I get to Purgatory,
& they might know
how to help me with the
mind thing.
They know
the problem — keep it moving &
praying *Don'tletSatangetin!*
PR **I** DE is the *greatest* sin.
Sister says,
PRIDE is **SATAN's**
SIN—
I guess it
is greatest be-
cause it is
SATAN's.

I'm scared
& I'm not even
sure what it *is*,
but Sister says

PRIDE is <u>So</u> Bad,
it'salways**Mortal.**

So I listen
closely   to what Sister says
in Religion. PRIDE is *Self-*
Importance & Self-Satisfaction,

Taking Pleasure
in what <u>You</u> have
done.

How lucky Sister is,
not only to be holy,
but an expert on sin.

Of course, if *she* said
that, or even just agreed
with me, she'd be *GUILTY*
of PRIDE

See how easily   you can
start taking
credit,   feeling so
confident   you could
lose all
humility &
forget about

GOD —

like what happened that August I
saved the boy who... *HelpmeLord!*

Italmostslippedout!

They were allaround
me, saying how good I was &
whataswimmer&aquickthinker
& not even scared& his Mom
was kissing me &crying &I was
believing them, saying ThankYou
&Thank You & *OhMyGOD!*

I forgot GOD!

*That's what **Satan** Did!*

Bad

We called a truce that Christmas
& I visited him
In Bristol, one dark bag
        filled with fancy dresses &
            rhinestone bracelets for my nieces
                hand knit socks & fruit cake,   two quarts each
                    of rye whiskey & cream.
                        We were good friends then.

It was the only time in our lives.

I made a huge bowl of eggnog, all of us
            in the long narrow kitchen, separating
                        eggs,   wildly laughing,
                    none of us able to keep
            our hands to ourselves.

It was a l w a y s that way with us:
    g r a b b i n g ,   s l a p p i n g ,   h o w l i n g .

                        That year he painted my portrait—
his studio an abandoned warehouse
        with patterned tin ceilings.
                A h u g e s p a c e with a warmcenter:
        the easel, the model's chair,
            green brocade worn down
                to the thick hemp veins
                    underneath,
                        the small table where he washed the brushes,
                    made peanut butter sandwiches &
                boiled the water at teatime.

Those were Brahms days,
                good Wagner days
                        listening to <u>Tannhauser</u>
                                while he painted
                        what he saw in my face.
                & there were rules—
        no makeup,
    hair in a stream over my shoulders.
                        I tried some blush one morning,   but he sent me back
        to wash.

                Two
                flights down was the toilet   &
                                there was always shame, him
                                        handing me the roll of paper,   cAckling
        as I closed the studio door.

    Two
        flights
            down
                & I could still hear the mad edge of his Laugh:
                        me having to pee so often, him
                                finding me asleep
                    once on the cot, nightgown at my hips,
                                butt stark naked
                                        in the moonlight.

He threw his head back HOWLing,
                VicToriOuS,
        each time he repeated that story.

And nobody laughed like he did:
                        m o u t h H U G E to his tonsils
                                        & the
                                        black
                                        tunnel
                                        of his
                                        throat,
                the vein
                just under
                his jaw bone
                b a l l o o n e d
                with p l e a sure
                l i k e a c o c k
                a w ak en e d
                f r o m   s l e e p,
                                        hisface heartattackred.

I was always so willing to do our mother's
        bidding. I see us hovering
                around her, "Why do you
                hate your sister?" she'd ask him
                                or to me, "It was the right thing to do"
                                        — report back to her
                                        when he was smoking.

Afternoons he'd be there   waiting
                                finishing his tea
                        & jellied toast.
                He wouldn't even let me take off my coat,
                                thr0wing me
                                down on the bed   then
                                daring me   to try to get up.
                With the tips of his fingers
                between my breasts, he'd
                                jab me & knock me
                                down again.

        There were days I'd lie there, refuse to get up,
        the way I refused that morning he forced me
                        into Mom's closet —
                                fat red
                                banana
                                curls the
                                length of
                                my arm
                                                        cut
                                        totheboneatthebaseofmyskull.

                        but he'd
                threaten to   punch me
                                if I didn't
                                get up
                                m y
                        B iG B rOT H eR
                        HUGE in the D O O R WAY,
                all juiced up
                                me rocking up

                                —
                                44

&
down
on the bed,
fingers pressing my vagina, the cold rush of
pee & the DAR**K** S T A I N of
S h **A** m e s p r e a d i n g t h r o u g h m y u n i f o r m

...   is a tunnel
inside my chest:
hot, tight, small
and **d**ark. Not
t o t a lly black,
e nough   gray
for me to see
the s h a d ows
I make a l o ne
here:the beaten
calf, theburned
b r a n c h e s,
the bruisedgrey
stone. No, it is
not enough for
Sad to sit here
qu i etly a lone
—content to be
left alone. No,
it must insist it
-self into every
place that j0y
lives or recalls.
G r e e d y
for something
so knotted &
small), it takes
m   o   r   e
than i ts share
at the table—
c o m p e ting

with each sun-
r i se or son's
cry.   I even
felt i t s t i r
and perchon
the backofmy
neck   when
my husband
drewthe ruby
n e c k l a c e
close&clasped
itbehindmyhair.
I t was Christ-
mas. & Sad
has s h a p es
& s m e l l s.
S o metimes
I can touch it.
S a d   i s
the h u g e
moss covered
b o o t of that
bl o a ted oak
plundering its
way through
the   farmer's
picket fence.
Sad is a too-
Tall GirL when
boys & her
brotherlaugh

& tease.
Sad is my
M o t h e r's
coldcreamed
face, when I
r e a c h u p
totouchit. Sad
is my father,
d r u n konce
in the bath-
room,mother
pounding on
the door.Sad
is my mother
s t i l l crying
on the couch.
It'swetsmelly
sheets; i t 's
kneelingatthe
bathtub'saltar
—wrists numb
intheicywater.
It's S i s t e r
Mary Thomas
saying I have
no backbone.
S a d is the
weddingring
I for get to
wear & the
flannel night

gown I re-
ly on in bed.
Sad is the
place that
secrets go;
It's the place
I go when
there's no
place else
tobesmall.

I cannot remember my body
before the hair:
dark frenzied
gateway
between
virtue   & sin.
It seemed that the body
had thrown on
its clothes.

Did the hair arrive
when Eve sinned?

Perhaps
there's a possible undoing:
return to pre-Eden
Eve & the hair
disappears.

Or
perhaps the hair
isn't shame
but nature's
protection

& like the thorn on holly
&   roses,

the hair
brings blood:

glory blood,
Eve blood,
Bread & Wine Blood.

This curtained kingdom
that generates
the blood then
releases it,
is the gate
through which
my son entered
the world.

What
holier
place
than this
vagina,
this cave
&birthplace
F o r c e d   O p e n
when he was full&
grown & it was
time for him to
m a ke his way
Out
like Christ did
on Easter Morning?

What holier sacrament
than the sex

he was made of
beneath this
flourish of hair?

The V at the body's center:
those who shrunk from it,   those who couldn't wait to
touch it.

I can't forgive You
for leaving me
so ashamed
before statues of naked women
I saw for the first time
at the Met.
Had these artists
sinned? I asked
Sr. Consolata.

How did it happen
that those darkened
tunnels became places
only Satan would visit?

Lord, was it *Y*our idea
to make it impure
to explore
what might have led to
another church door?
Later, I did penance
for the magicthatshotthrough
mybellywhen I discovered
the vagina.
Lord, how *could* You
give Your child over to
nuns who'd teach me—
Never be proud of it,
always be afraid of
thesinthat overtakes me
at the movies   when a coupleon the screen
kiss
too long.

Desperate to diffuse the excitement,
                    I'd tightenthelipsofmyvagina,   but
          the tight-ening
   caused   rock
                -ing   which I do
          until now
                    when I have to
          pee.

                    Maybe that's what   the peeing is for —
                              to protect me
                         from that wish between my legs. Later,
                              I learned about
                                   women
                                   lovingwomen& I was
                                        afraid.   Remember how I struggled
                         for weeks in therapy
   (I was already almost thirty)   before confessing
                    the dream about Helene &
                                                            the Sky
                                        crowded
                                   with
                                             Breasts
          Glorious Breasts,

                    Godmothers & generous feeders
                         someday of a son —
   yet should *I* long to suck them,
          to nestle my face
                between   them,   know the   rise of
                                        the nipple
                                   to my tongue
                                   with its shy, eager
                                   answers, then finally
                              find the milk & drink it &
          I have blasphemed.

How then is this body different

from that mountain regaled in Emerald Suit & White
Turban?

Shall I spend my life with downcast eyes?

The cat on my lap
pulls
my
left
hand
down to his neck   insisting his shoulders
& face
want
touching   just as the dark part
of my belly &
sex

want themselves in his touch.   But

priests & nuns,
the holiest of noblest
of teachers,   deprive& punish
thebody   for its greedy appetites

rather than f e e ding & P a *R* a d ing it as a TrophY, another of God's Jobs Well Done

taking its place
on the podium

next to the Soul,   or those Pinedressed Peaks,   or that Cattail.

Are they suggesting that

GOD

(in His frailty)

failed

in His role of   Father of the Universe:

investing pleasure
in something as flimsy
as the body?

Yet if God is, (& I understand He is)
& is therefore
capable of any perfection,

why would He sculpt us
in any less
perfect gesture?
Why create color, like the
redgolds of hair & flesh & Maple Crown Roses,
if He didn't intend to
seduce our eyes?
Was He naïve & ill-advised?   Or just
cruel: teasing us
to whet our appetites,
then slapping our faces when we'd respond?

Since a part doesn't recognize
itself
until it is touched,
perhaps
it is not shallow   but holy
to use these fingers
to touch myself
as freely as I touch this cat or rose?
Perhaps then,
it is <u>not</u> a sin to T h r o w this B U T T   or L *i* p s   or
THighs   into that circle
of eyes

as   Another Masterpiece of His Invention.

What we need is

m o r e time
in front of
the mirror,   not less.
We might learn
the language of the organs,
hearing as they speak: then exhorting them
to Demandtheir share.

_____

55

Let my body   take a lesson
              from that lion paRading there
                  who, trusting itself,
                      needs no invitation or permission,
                                              mane as important
                                                  as eyes,
              eyes a signal   of the wiLd,   perfect
                              terrain of its Soul,   &
    come Out
      of hiding
              to shed its clothes
                in front of
              the mirror,   palms delighting in the f u l l
                      S w e l l of H I P
                  that place where the Belly
                                      bows
                                      down
                                      before
                  the warmdarkforestofhair.

              Nothing more delicious than a rib or
                              hip
                          insisting
                          it
                          -self
                                      through this
    banquet of Flesh. Fingertips to Nipple,   Navel,   Lips, I touch   each
                      earthened
                      shape,   picturing myself
                      as a   girl unattended,
                                      searching
                  the   mystery
                          of her
                          dark
                          slim
                          soul.

The only way I can take you back, Lord
is if we agree   that you're just
another parent:
well-intentioned of course,   but
                                        flawed   like the rest of us.
Either you've been too Self-important
                or your nuns just misrepresent you
        as a cruel God   who rejects his children
for wanting some portion of pleasure that does not include him.

            Why would eating the apple,
            (a child saying *No, Dad,*
            I must do it my way,)
            cause such an uproar?
                                    What parent doesn't understand
                                that   for a child to grow
        she must test the ground she walks on?

What father wouldn't understand *this* daughter's
            need to be good &
        to please & wouldn't
        reassure her?
                    Why let her suffer?   Why would you
                                        entrust her to nuns
                                            who'd applaud
                                            when she rejects
                                        her body's smoothness
        to honor you?
                Why would you want your child to hurt?
                What would you say if I did that to *my* son?

                Where is your human kindness?

                                    Why set such a glorious feast,
                            served on the table   at the center of
                                        these legs, &
    refuse me entry?
    Why season it with sensations

if the feast is reserved for
conception?

You know as well as I do   that there's no need to
add orgasm   or that absolute astOnishment
when that dark hallway is discovered & traveled.

Sexual pleasure is superfluous in baby making.

We'd participate in the act
& bear the labor
without the Ecstacy—

a Child is Gift enough.
Pleasure enough.

Surely, *You* know that.

The Cage

The first time I break my ankle, I am   eight months pregnant &
nowhere near ready to let go,   fierce with fear as I am of this child,   already   so much   more
important   than I am or anyone else for that matter,
this greatest of all possible
judges: greater even
than the Church.

But what if I can't love him?

What if I don't even like him?

He'll be there with me for the rest of my life.

In the middle of *my* life,
a child
takes over   where Christ left off   reminding me   that I am less
& his rights
count—   not mine.
His will be done.
I have no power here.
He will be born.   He will split my body   in   two   when
he decides & I'll be
thrown   into yet another life where his life
occupies
mycenter.

Still I cannot direct it   more than   a few minutes, then
I'll have to step aside & let him go again
when he decides
as if he weren't just as vital as   any other organ in my body   or limb.

Eleven years later to the day,   I leave his lesson
hating him for not caring   enough
about the music,
not wanting for himself
what I want, talking instead about Burger King & I love you, Mommy, kissing up to me

to   quiet me,   caring only that I not be angry,   changing the subject   as if it were possible
that any other life but his music & my disappointment   could exist now between us.
                                                                                        But

                    I have to shut my mouth.

                    I have no power here.

        I cannot tear into him,   cannot make him love the music   as much as I do.

            So soon   he's flown out from the center of me.
                                                        Let him go.
            Let him go,   a mother's mantra instructs me
                            as I start down the stairs,
                                                him almost at the door, chatting on
            about Whoppers & Chicken Tenders & Our Special Day &   I'm
                doing it   saying nothing,   not interrupting   for the thrill of
            even the smallest chastisement,   but I miss   the   last
                                                                step,
                                                                    my ankle
                                                    turns in
                                                    on itself,   my
                                                    whole body
                                                    smashes down
                                                    on top of it,   DAggers of L I G H T
                    s p l I t   m y   b o d y   I n   2.   *F U   C K!*   I   scr Eam into the
lobby of this Jewish Community Center where children walk with violins & backpacks & *D A   V*
I d! when   someone offers   water,   *D   A   V   I   D!*   It's black again,
        then The Police   then
                            David   yelping "Mom! I'mhere!"

Pain is the cage I can't climb out of.   It's the only life I feel
these four months   since I missed my step, fell&
                                                fractured &
dislocated
                              my left ankle: three bone groups
                              hopelessly
                              broken,
                                                        then pieced togetherwithpins plates&
screws.

                              Then some surgeon   (or even
nature)
slipped   & now the skin burns   like singed tar
          with R.S.D.: Reflex Sympathetic Dystrophy.
                                                At night, it's only the *PAI* N,
                    nothing to distract me
          the way daylight distracts
                                offering   some small
                    distortion to startle me
                              like the promise of a shampoo
                                        or   my son
                    playing a Seitz concerto when he really   means it
          or a chocolate bar   or movie   or any other   tenderness
                                                from my   husband.
But night takes everything away:
                                        itsqueezeslife
                                        downtopain,   f i l l i n g   TheDar**K**
                    with the foot's   unforgiving
                                        burning.

                    Is this the FiRe of Hell?

                                                And people aren't kind in the dark:
          nurses & husbands   expect to be   left alone.
          They pretend they don't hear you.   They've given   more than their   share
                                        in daylight.
                                                They expect you to sleep.

But pain doesn't sleep.
It never closes its eyes.

                                                    So I am grateful for this
                gift of morphine;
        I know the glory of it: that nothing hurts for awhile   nothing   moves
    nothing   peaks or
                        keeps its shape.   On morphine
    l i f e   s l   o   w   s   to a   thin grey line   on a   machine.   Bless us, O Lord.

Each time I ask that my prescription be filled
or my bandages changed,   I risk   another
raised brow or rolling eye: that familiar flash of SHIT! Not *aGain*!
that husband or son   being closest   feel free enough to show.

Lives here are built on doing for ourselves
then helping each other.
But now there is no balance.
Meals must be served, hair washed, X-
Rays, physical therapy & surgeon appointments need chauffeuring.

Now the foot is the most important member of the family.
It's a second baby to me,
but unlike my first who is
strOng&hardy,
this one's frail: its mottled skin purple& red as   a terrible mistake.
Cranky, fretful,   demanding attention that
no one else could get away with,
it's never satisfied.
It uses me,
laughs&makes me ask for things that shame me,
so I do without
the 4 A.M. Percoset&
cover the bedpan with paper towels.   *I'm Sorry*,   I say
too often,
ThAnk

You...

I

Love   You....
Would   it   be
possible...?
I   wonder...

I'm   SORRY...   I'm
SO
Very

Sorry.

Nobody lets you complain.
*You must be **P**atient. Think Positively.*
Attitude determines cure.
Interpretation: Lie.
Say,   "Fine.
Coming along just fine."   Smile
when people ask   about your smashed foot.   Collect all
the unsightly rage&
self-pity, electrical shocks&
insidious burning
&stuffthem
downyour
throat   the way we women used to
stuffunsightlyhips&
buttsintorubberized
girdlesthatkept us   from moving.
Once inside the narrowed tunnel of your throat,
P**ai**n rAge & Self*P*ity
will mergeintoone subcutaneousconstruction.
Hold it tightly until it s w e l l s enough
for you to feel it
whistling as you breathe; though
when itthickenssomuchit
threatenstochokeyou,
s h o v e I t
further down. Keep it
lodged in your belly
like an alien fetus that
devours you   from the inside
out.   Everyone knows
if you can't see it, it's not there
Every six or eight weeks though,   just for the hell of it,
boilover&vomit it all over your family,
*You can take my **f**uckin' ankle*
with all its fuckin' whining
& shove it up your Fuckin' Ass!

Then cut the ears off well meaning friends
& patronizing doctors.

Spit at the next one who laughs.
You can tear your clothes off now
    or stand on the street corner flailing your crutches
                                    or collapse in a puddleofpiss&tears on the floor.
    No one will try to stop you,
                unkempt as you are
            with all your shitty virtue.
                    Nobody appreciates a Mess.

The machine went into SP*ASM* when he
STUCK the needle into the Peroneal Nerve
atthebaseofmytoes.
*Diff*use *Sensory Neuropathy*: my disease is
a puffed up combination of
consonants snapped.
Nobody knows if life will return
to my foot. I dreamed
he'd find the culprit:
a small pin imprudently placed
that shorted everything out.
But diffuse says
there's no culprit to blame:
nothing to explain
the buZZing, the constant *BUZZ*ing & electrical ShOCKs &
toes that feel like sandpaper
wrapped around blocks of wood.

"To spread as f l u i d,"
the dictionary reads. So air or sky, universe or pain,

diffuse
means allover everywhere cannot be caught or collected beginning & end
somewhere beyond this border of skin & bone
like a virus that slips quietly in,
leaves its terrible f i l m o f d i s e a s e,
imperceptible
until the land is in ruins.
D i f f u s e.

Nothing more they can do.

If this is the way I pay my dues,   I   will
-ingly offer this ankle.
If none of us escape unscathed,
some part lawfully   shattered &   broken
by
God's Great Need to keep us,   & balance
who gets with   who gives,
if this is the way He   chooses
to run His Store,   I'll go along
more than a little guilty   for the lightnessof my bill,
relieved that He's taken   only an ankle
instead of a heart,   a breast,   my son.
Thankful
for my lesser   sentence, I will   take my
small portion   of pain, cradle this bruised ankle
babe   in my palms, &   croon it
asleep:
a preferred child.
And like the preferred child
who gets the easiest chore in the house
(a chore, of course,   suggesting a semblance
of His fairness,   but a perfunctory one
like dusting the furniture),   while others are assigned to   scrub
floors   or the oven,   I quietly polish the piano,   then tend to the fire.

Truce

Forced to listen to the body's sentence
as it hesitates &faults, you learn to
trust its limitations

Even love isn't enough.

Now even our coming together
in the first place gets questioned.

It's like that at Fifty.

I'm thinking again
about B i g things —
Happiness & Peace
— no longer vague,
they take on
a muscularity,
a defined
shape
like a chest or a back
that starts with a feeling
that t h i c k e n s
in the belly then Pushesup
into the biceps finally
collecting
at the bend
in the throat.
Life crystallizes
&we're not looking
so much for higher purpose but nuts & bolts:

I have it or I don't.

That's where we are now.

Our love I take for granted. Strange as it seems, it's gravy.

73

At the end   the mouth   makes its choice:
                    to
                    drop
                        or holdup.
                    Hers d
                          o
                          v
                          e,
            no struggle there
                    just an

                            a
                            r
                              c
                                turnedswiftly d
                                               o
                                               w
                                               n
                                               w
                                               a
                                               r
                                          d
            towards the
                    h   u   g   e
                    s w o   l   l
                    e   n   l e g s
                    t h a t   remind
                    m   e   of my
                    h u s   band's
                    f   a   t h e r.
    The color of his ankles
            marked
            his passage,
    traced his dying
                step
                    by
            measured
                    step.

74

All the plugged up life
                    j u i c e s
               f i nall y l e t g o p o u r e d
     fromheadchestwhole upper body left him
                                                   frail,
                         almost
                               weightless;
                                        then rushedthrough
                                        hislegstohisankles
                              before drainingintothedirt.

               What *does* happen   when the body
     finally   dies?
                         .
                              Do the legs let
                              go of the water
                              like a woman
                              full with birth?

               Where
          do the gasses
            go, the tears
                the piss &theblood?

                              Does the w a ter
                         b   u   r   s t through the
                              w eak e n e d skin
                                        drenching the body in its
                                        second amniotic fluid outside the
                                        cocoon of flesh? Is that
                                        what it's for: to
                                        wash the body
                                        into the earth the way
                                        it washed the baby
                                        into the world?

Raked out of the earth
by forensic anthropologists,
bone b i t s & teeth
are all that is left of
her daughter,
missing these 13 years.

She insists
that she   see them   & he
arranges   the de lic ate   frag ments
each   in   its
place   on
                                the   white
                        cloth.

Alone now, she
moves through the dark
fingering her rosary. Then,
like a priest addressing the Eucharist,
she
bends
over the table,
puts her cheek to
the chalk cool plate
that was once the
forehead, then
dips
her
mouth
intotheblack
cup of
cheek,   &   with   the   tips   of
        her   fin   gers,   she   tra-
        ces   each   piece,   the   sli
        ver   of   rib   bits   of
        hip   thumb   the   cru-
                shed   wrist,

caressing each
s e a r c h i n g for
a familiar lift
or
turn
that will finally tell her,
like the particular
shape of a
head
.... Removing her shawl,   she places it over the
pieces of bone,   &climbs onto the table
curlingherbodytowardsher onlychild.

She wraps her arms
a r o u n d what remains
of her   life.

*What part of the body
do you reject?*

the masseuse asks.
Behold my
6
foot
tall
and
angry
back,

some discs still
s c r e a m i n g like
c o l i c k y
babies
while others, quiet &
capable no longer
of speech,
despair of all hope of recognition.
Exhausted from decades of

bend-
ing &
twist
-ing
to
accommodate,
now a n g r y discs
ROAR, r e f u s i n g to
give in. Long since tired of
pleading for some
muscled mother
to defend & protect it,
the b u t t finally
d
r
o   p   s
in
d E
feat.

I'd like this war
to be over: no more
insidious   battles
scored
beneath
the surface.

Having spent Life
dutifully   ignoring
&   Abhorring you,   My Body,
I promise you m o r e
attention. I will no longer
avoid places no
good Catholic would travel,
nor will I shave your head of
its   F l o u r i s h   o f   H   A   I   R.

Past
D A y l i g h t Sa v i n g s   T i m e,   the   days
areshorternow
but I vow to protect
every   dribble of Sun.
Admiring my back
in the mirror,   I wrap   my arms
around each perfect bump&
scar,
My Prodigal Children;
I'm sorry, I say.

It's your turn.

My soul
can

step aside.

I do God's work here.

People bring their marriages,   saints & demons, mothers & fathers,
the cloaks of their shame.

Catholic
remnant   I live here   performing Works of Mercy: feed the hungry,   clothe the naked,
visit the sick,   bury the dead— & free will:

the bottom line that will throw out every commandment.

Frankly,
I'm grateful.   It's the saving grace of the Church.

Brought up on Thou Shalt Not &
Mortal Sin,

I float safely
now   through all nuns habits, knowing   the last judgement
was always   infineprint: the asterisk
at the bottom of every doctrine:

let your conscience be your guide.

Let's face it, every religion has its Advantages: huManity,   FLA**I**R,   *Abraham*
negotiating
with God   as an equal.

But conscience is the final God:
if you believe you are right, then you're right;
if you believe you are wrong, you are wrong.   So

this time
I rewrite history
placing the baby before Him, emptying the Church of all Pharisees:
nuns, priests &self-proclaimed
prophets
of doom.

No dogma here,
lust & pride are no longer deadly.   Saints & angels loosen their halos.
I once expected vaulted ceilings,
a long

                        climb
                        up the
                        steps
                        to the
                        Massive Bronze Door.

                                              Once holy only on dark afternoons,
        now Church is   all small
                goodnesses   like one's home,
                                    or a father's favorite chair,
                                    a book of Joyce's stories
                                                    or a violin safe in a velvet lined box.

                        And anyone who wishes can be Jesus:
                Perhaps
        Chekhov is
                Jesus   & Brahms & da Vinci,   the midwife & yogi, the altar boy, soldier & cantor....
                        Godparents all,
                                        I place the baby among them,
                        pour the water,   anoint &   free her
                                                of all past promises.

        She is clean;
        she is warm.

                        So the scaffolding is gone:
                        I don't go to Church,
                                        can't even say I believe.   Saints & Lucifer
                                                    seem preposterous to me now,
                                        though the residue at the bottom of
                                        the wine glass remains.

                        My hands have gotten old:
                        freckled with spots
                like a nun's or a priest's.

                                Skin is l a x, loses flexibility,
                                                finally
                        falls into its

                                        ───
                                        81

inevitable map

                      with thousands

        of thresholds
      to be balanced on,

                           wavered at,

                                 then

flung
  into   or

        from,   r a v a ging   still   another piece   of my soul.

The beach seems used up this morning.

It's like that after an overripeSaturday: mesh trash cans full with half eaten watermelon,
beer cans, gum wrappers &coffee cups.

I like it like this: the morning after
used &adored.   Like a bed after l0ve:
scraps of   what was
important,   pieces of
pleasure

strewn,
affectionate
&harsh.

& it lets itself   be played with:

a speed boat skims a long   the   top
like   a gull   s a i l i n g a   whale,
the surfers & joggers are here,
a woman in dreadlocks
bends her
back to the sun,

gull tracks   l ook like
miniature   bows &
arrows   or
sailboats
or
kites

in
the   sand.

A woman walks alone

by the jetty:
her hair is frenzied,   grey,   her hips & biceps,
thick,
familiar.

Together she's   another   perfect
smiling I'll bet
creature in a turquoise sarong,
& collecting   seashells.

I come here for sOund as well as for Motion: the Ocean
Rolling Closerlikesome Great GrandFather   who speaks   & his voice is A l i v e &
Forever   in a house: r e a ching into the pipes &
floorBoards ,   then   R   I   S   I   N
G   like a s t e a d y   stream of Safe air.   When you hear it,   you   know
you are   safe
& afraid.

Some call it T h u n d e rous,   the Voice of this Ocean:
more Booming perhaps   likeamute on a horn   or drum
that pales the music just enough, lets us
breathe for awhile.

And it's like that with lovers: the mute
needed,
after the heat
takes the breath   & keepsit

suspended.

Sometimes I think   the only sane way to conduct a marriage
is four days on, three days off —
a few days of mute   (talk of love
limited to the phone,
no sex maybe,)   pay bills, watch movies.

Stay away from the heart & the crotch.
Live somewhere between the Child &   the Stone.

When I think of all I obsess about, it's V   a   s   t ness,

Vastness & Isolation: e   n   d   l   e   s   s   Isolation—
e n d l e s s   O   c   e   a   n
rolling inside my chest,
smashing against it, making me small again, the way
Beethovenmakes me small   & holy. The

endless sound of O c e an *B u I L D I N G U P,* then
thr**O**wing
      itself away
            on the beach, always spent, always
                   g *a* t hering steam the 0 cean
   repeating itself, rising &

       dying,
           dying & R i s *i* n G.

    It's the only God I can believe in.

Glory

It's the only thing that survives out   here   where the s U n &   w *I* nd
scorch
everything
    in sight.   These dunes are sacred;
                            Sunday mornings, I should do my praying
                                    here.
            Black Pine,   broad
                            &deep:
        as any other   icon   I've lived by,
                                                PUSHed,   Bullied,
    tormentedby the *WIND*   while the SUN sits   High,
                            harsh &   adoring.

                    I love how
            this   Tree,
                            fists   thrOwn   out
                            to defend it,
        Holds Its Ground,   like any Life   or Body
                    that knows
                            it's entitled.
                    & I love the twist of it
            — the sometimes
                        u g l y
                        t
                            w
                        i
                            S
                        t—
        never bothered by beauty,
                    sculpting
                    its own   body
                            from the   D a n c e
            of its   B A T T L E
                    WithThe   W *I ND.*

89

ANOTHER LIFE

After a hysterectomy

                                        Not so much as slightly interested
in any higher purpose,   I'll be content to be
                        perfect
                              in body:
                            a sculpture
                            of myself,
                                        some days all male: full chested,
                                        muscular, with legs & ass that
                                    b u l g e   &   pOp
                                        where they should.

            I'll be cool,
        unaffected &
                    somewhat disinterested;
                                        the hair on my legs will be
                                                    soft & tan &
                    just enough of it   will curl
                                with pleasure of its own accord.
                                My eyes too   will be
        pleased as blue cryStals
                                as   I   leapfor theLob   or   the   goaL   Line
or wallow in self   pleasure—   the   pull   of   Wing   Bones   V
AU L Ting   when   I   butterfly   a   cross   the   pool.

            I'll love the cool strip
                    when I stand before the woman,
                        nude as silk,
                                    waiting   for the rIsing
                        that will take place.
                    I won't abuse her
                                        & I'll love
        being taken;   I'll want what she can do for me
                    & be grateful.
                        Though when I need her,
                            the woman in me   will   rise   up
        more nearly perfect,   fill out in   my skin,
                                shaping mounds
                                    of down deliciousas

                                    sin,
                                  nipples
                              s w e l l i n g
                              for the touch.
                                              Somedays   I'll be Martha Graham
                                    slight & female
          with   legs & fingers that leaptomyeverycommand &
                                                      there will be no part of
                                                      me that I cannot touch
     or fathom.   I'll know how
                    my eyes feel
                                  in their   w i d e   sockets.
                                                        I'll dilate my pupils at will,
                              render my skin   wet or dry,
                                                    I'll
                                                  know
                                                      the twist of
                                                  a tongue,
                    the nauseated taste of a
                    tooth turning bad,
                                        the hiss in an ear listening to Mozart.

                                                                  There'll be m o r e to
                                                            my body than a belly
                                                growling with   hunger
                                                or a pussy wet with
                                                            want
                                                            or a bowel or
                                                            bladder too full:
     a l l   o r g a n s   w i l l   s i n g   o u t   d   l   i   r   i   o   u   s —
                                        a   ca co ph o ny of
                                                      partspushingtheirwayto
                                    themike-liverlarynxesophagusappendix even
              uterus *ghost*   delivering their own sweet
                                              *mus*ics: the spleen
                                                  making its racket,
                    my0varies,   saved for *lullabies* & d i r g e s.

Rummaging in the attic for feathers, my Angel

drags a box from the closet,

We'll be seagulls! she says.

Like roller skates or a driver's license,

Angels increase possibilities.

So I gather my skirts,
spin full circle on my toes
as she   dances in
front of   the
mirror
in   S h A p E s   from other days —

the leathered hut
of a turtle's back,   a bright red beard & handlebar mustache
a horse's worn shoes,
a bag of sweetened bones.

From the box marked   FACES,   ASSORTED SKINS   &
HAIR, she chooses   Feathers —   grey & white,   a   few   Black,   &
measuring   my   a r m   s   p   a   n & the B R E A D T H of my chest,
she   a r r a n g e s   the   f e a t h e r s
i n a *f a n* o n the f loor, grey up top,
the *SH*O*CK* of WHITE
underbelly,
a   black
angle

where a hand would be,
one small diamond
at the
tip.

Then polishing our beaks

in front of the mirror,
she tucksourlegsup
into our thighs.

At the beach, we b a t h e in a black rubber tire, *F L **a** p* ping
sea water like perfume on our wings & toes....

Then   S k A t i n g   U   p   o

-v e r the beachhouse,   we summon the guLLs —

those *d a v ening* Wings!

G   u   l   l   s

of   al l   S   I   z   **E** s

d
i
v
e

in trash
cans
for fish
or   birds   or
bread
or   Stand Still Fully Satisfied
breasts puffed with peace.

We
d
a
n
ce
over a
lame dog's
head;
now   H *I* G h above the white caps,

the Conductor's Baton,

we are   the white violin,
r   *i*   s i n g
&
fall
-ing,

S h*A* ping the   l   o   n   g   l   i   m   b   of   the   S   o   n   g

———
93

Take for instance this African Violet bl o o ming its brains out the tenth year in a row:
shameless in purple— scores of furious faces & voluptuous leaves. Like me,
surrounded by its family, it's just h**a**ppy here
sitting in its white pot
in the middle of its Family r*oo*m.

& like us, all our plants
have had children:
the pencil cactus has three, two fully grown, one toddler,
the yuka, just one,
the fiddle leaf ficus, false aralia & rubber   more than we can count —
just ridiculous in their rushtooutd**o**.

Once upon a time a man,   a woman & a boy
were so delirious in love
with the woods,   that they
wantedthemcloser, sothey
built a house in the
heart of
the pines.   Then

begging the woods
indulgence   they asked for   a few trees: a small rubber perhaps,
some fern,
a dracena.
But these
g r e w
TALLer, so
the man, the woman   & the boy
built a greenhouse, an A t r i u m
at the Heart of the house: a
H U G E   R O O M
with Skylights & Walls of Glass &
old brick & lots of cold well water.

Once inside
the P l a n t s   S t r e t c h e   d   O   u   t   &   Up,

                                                                        but complained,
    theylikecrowdingleavestouching,Hovering even.   So the family   went outside,
dug pine, hemlock, flowering plum & filledtheroomtocrowding.
                                        They invited the birds:

                        c a r d i n a l s
                                                            came,
    some
                b l a c k   c r o w s.

                                                & they made no attempt
                                            to domesticate their trees
                                                with tea tables & wicker sofas,
                                            only a rocker or two
                        & a small bench for the child.

before the bath

my son strips   f l ings
                                    sneakers
jeans
                                                sweatshirt
        they
                        parachute
                        like
                        strange
                            B
                    i
                            r   d
                s
        dan
        gle
        from a lamp
                                    the desk
            a sock
            from   the ear of   My Pet MOnster   then he
    caws   some   w i l d g e E se song   H i g h- piTched   V i c T O r i o u S
    as he   w
        h
        i   r   l s   through   the   house   Be*a*ting   his NaKed BuTT
                        I remind him
                        the bath will be cold.   He quickens   SQU*EAL*s
LOUDer   T HR*UST*s his
        HIPS   in my direction   Giggling   as   he   watches   his   penis   re spOnd
                        then he
                        lowers
                        him
                        -self   gently   into   the w a ter,
                                                r
                                                o
                                                l
                                                l
                                                s

        on   his belly — his   long *n*arrow body almoststr O n g,
                his tight butt   already Beautiful.

Somedays I don't even wash my face   or brush my teeth. I love the
undisturbed
crustofsleep   that collects
                in the corners
                of my eyes,   remnants of the deep drape
                                 that w r a p p e d my body
                                 all night in my own bed   like the arms of my Mother
              —not her really,
                    but the broad Gesture of Mother
                    that each of us crave& keep   as icon
                    in the safe crib   of our hearts.

              I don't even mind if you don't love me now.
        I will again
        tomorrow   perhaps, but not
                    this morning
                    with grace   spill ing the sun's e x cess   over   paper s   & books
                                                   carelessly
                strewn
                            on the bed   as if it
                                                   knows
                                                            they belong here
                like a   hip,   a   thigh,   a   wash   of   hair,   or a
        fist   remembering
                            — a child's perhaps,
                    clutching mother's
                        forefinger   in that sign of   final   trust.

        The mother that loves me deepest   sleeps beside me,   sleeps
                                                                   inside
                                                                   me
                            in this Big *Bed*.

It's the basic flaw of nature: not to be able to take another point of
view.   All jammed up in
               -side this package of
               skin, bones, muscles,
               & driven by lots of
               water, the ever-giver,
               we can not step
                                                                        outside
                                                even for a moment
to take off
         this
             flesh,   don a
                  trunk,   t h r O w   green   or
                                              even
                                                 dead
                                              leaves,   T o s s
                                              a   F
                                                      r

                                                                 E
                                                        n
                                                           z
                                                        y
                            of
               branches
                                                                into
                                                      the
    S k y.

Let there be commerce between us, Whitman says.

                                                       So I clip my toenails
                                                       & pack my bag.

          I'll try the woods
                    this time: try living with the ants,   squirrels &   racoons,
          spiders &   other mavens:
                                        try acting natural

                                        with a buck
            nibbling at my ear & me a
                                    pear
                                    tree
                                    l
                                    e
                                    a
                                    k
                                    -ing
                                        Sap
                                        in
                                          its
                                        hair.
                                                            If you want,
        I'll be happy.

                But sometimes what we want we cannot have.

            Though why not?   Look at All
    the other things   in nature
    that trade places:
                            l i g h t
            becomes dark,   water
                                            hangs
                        invisible
                            in the air
        or freezes in a slab on a stone.   A   S i a mese   *F l y i n g   F I s h*
                                                divides its time equally

                                                    between water & air.   But
                perhaps this is the Pride the Priests talked about:

Lucifer's Pride.   *Bless me Father,*
                    I think I might have sinned.   The   l   o   n   g   t   a   i   l   of S I N
                                                                    follows me
            through   the   W o o ds   p a st   the   b u r ned   l eaves.
                Maybe someday
                        I'll know what sin is

                                    ___
                                    99

or know it isn't.

But now I grow out of

the ground with God   so I am captured

here by what might be

beyond.   Christ lives inside my whole: crawls

through

every

cra ck   in the dirt,

makes me

crossmylegs,   drinks my water,   sleeps in my bed,   Steps Up

to the refrigerator.

Even stepping on ants can be criminal where I believe,   where

pulling a

hat

down

rakishly

over an eye

can be cause for

shAme.

Using the body for anything but the Ghost   can kill you:

the Body Temple

is another receptacle for God

with no purpose of its own

or pleasure.

How strange

this God I

came up on: spreading fields & pastures, mountains, rivers & forests   that

extend   still   further,   yet   from   such   b o u n d l e s s n e s s,   a person

must keep

an

arm's

length

away.

But listen, God—

(You have such a strange name—practically good*.)*

Let there be

100

commerce between us.   Let's you and I finish the job.   Perhaps
the
   spine
   of
that
black
   pine   could trade places with mine, &   my skin could become leaves, &
          ears pine cones, &
                        blood fresh cool water.   Inviting that cypress
                                   to watch the sunrise
                              on the Hudson,
            I'd send   the desert to cool off
                     in the rain forest   & seduce a birch
                            in front of the fire.
                     I'd be a
                            bon
                            -sai   for a day, a month, maybe
   a year   & the marrow of that Japanese Maple
                                   could spend a splendid afternoon
         r o a m i n g   through   my   bones.   As
                                   rosewood or mahogany,
         or buffed raw oak,   I'd be a dining
                            table,   a *fiddle*,
                                                            a ladder
                  or a floor
        laying myself bare
                              for elbows, toes, fingers &paws &
                     the pattern
            of my
         grain
                     would be   another
                            perfect   story.   I'd remember
the forest & the
             slice of a knife,   the chainsaw & tarp,

                                   the long road down from the factory
            to here.

IOI

ACKNOWLEDGMENTS

Thank you to the editors of the journals in which these poems, some in different versions, first appeared.

Agni: "Glory"

Calliope: "Gravy"

Confrontation: "Family"

Feminist Studies: "Between Parents" and "before the bath"

Journal of New Jersey Poets: "Sad," "A Portrait of a Woman and the Shadow of a Man," "Prayer Outside the Church," "In the Mirror / At the Beach," "In This Big Bed"

Kaleidoscope: "Apology" and "Another Apology"

Kalliope: "Another Life"

Lip Service: "At the End of the Road towards Montauk: The Black Pine"

Madison Review: "Portrait of a Truce"

Moving Out, A Feminist Literary & Arts Journal: "The Cage"

Negative Capability: "Pageant of Rages," "The Body Complains," "The Only God"

Painted Bride Quarterly: "The Break," "Mess," "Easy"

Poetry East: "Perfect"

Rhino: "The Mother: Argentina, 1989"

Wisconsin Review: "To Here"

Special thanks to the Ragdale Center for the Arts for two residencies during which many of these poems were written.

SPECIAL THANKS

The birthing of GlOrious represents gifts from many generous friends & teachers. Special thanks to:

First & foremost, Alan, for urging me twenty years ago to find something for myself, involving no other, & since then, for supporting me in every way as I did that—from spearheading family vacations at Frost Place to providing pockets of time for me to go off alone & write.

David, my son, whose ideas provoke me & whose passion inspires me.

Siv Cedering, Robert Long, and Allen Planz—my East Hampton teachers those first years.

Donald Sheehan, in particular, and The Frost Place for providing that safe & holy place where I learned to write poems & years later returned to teach. There I found, for the first time, many of my dearest/wisest poet/friends.

David Keller for reassuring me that there's no way to avoid being a beginner when learning to write.

Stephen Dunn for accepting me into his workshop (sight & work unseen) purely on the strength of my zeal.

Galway Kinnell who taught me where to look to find the poem.

Louis Simpson who introduced me to Chekhov & the beautiful language of everyday speech.

Allen Ginsberg for saying, "The only way to write good poems is to write bad ones."

Molly Peacock who taught me to trust my subject matter and my words and my impulses with both. I have her to thank for my poems.

Baron Wormser who wondered about my devotion to the left margin, thereby releasing me to my impulse to roam in a poem.

Afaa Michael Weaver whose generous Foreword expresses such profound care and involvement with the work.

Karen Chase & Carol Snyder, girlfriends & unwavering supporters of GlOrious & me.

My many other generous friends—poets and civilians—who read these poems in their many configurations: Catherine Breitfeller, Andrea Carter Brown, Horty Carpentier, Teresa Carson, Sondra Gash, Ida Green, Syd Lea, Howard Levy, Maida Rosenheck, Maureen Seaton, Jack Wiler, Sandi Wisenberg, Baron Wormser, Michelle Wyrebek & Carole Yus.

Raphael Attias for design, Peter Cusack for composition & Carlos Andrade for his brilliant art piece that so expresses the themes central to GlOrious.

Florenz Greenberg & the staff of CavanKerry, for their intelligence, honesty & commitment to this book.